Read-Al

Phonics Stories

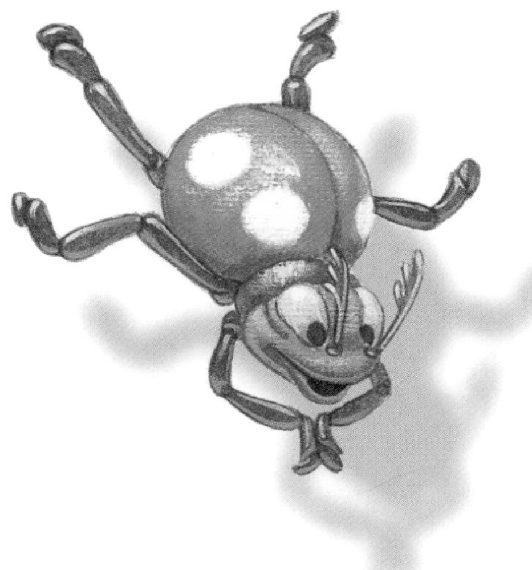

HAMPTON-BROWN

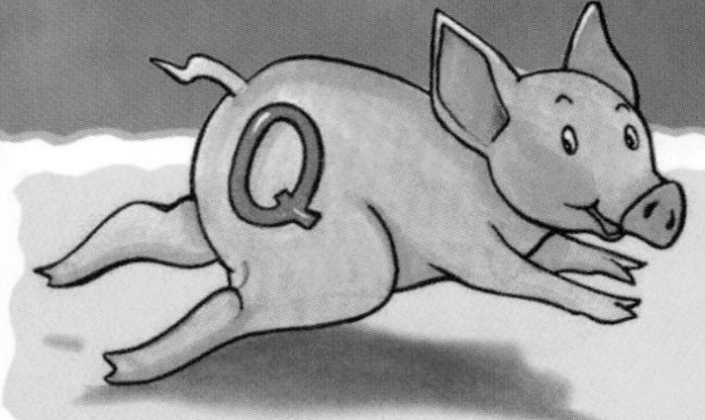

Contents

Tap, Tap
Sheron Long
© Hampton-Brown
8

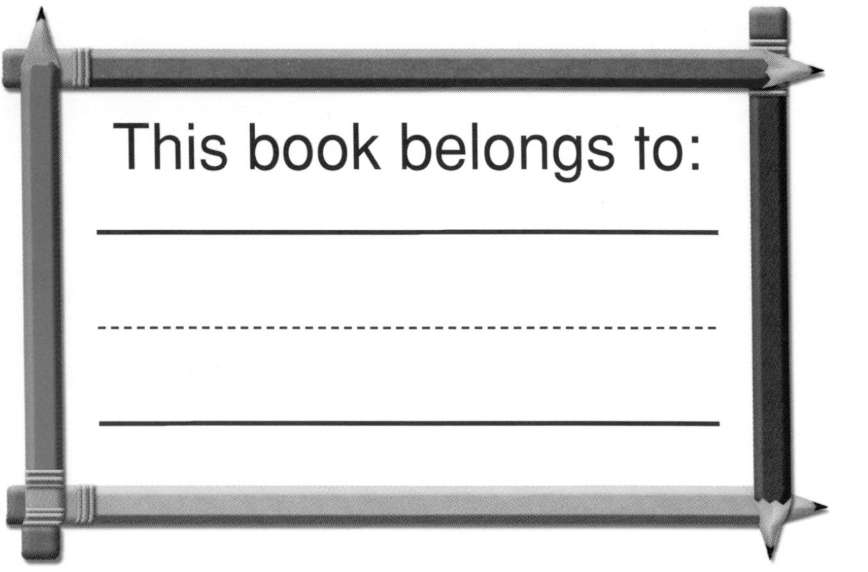

This book belongs to:

The cats sat.

Tap tap.

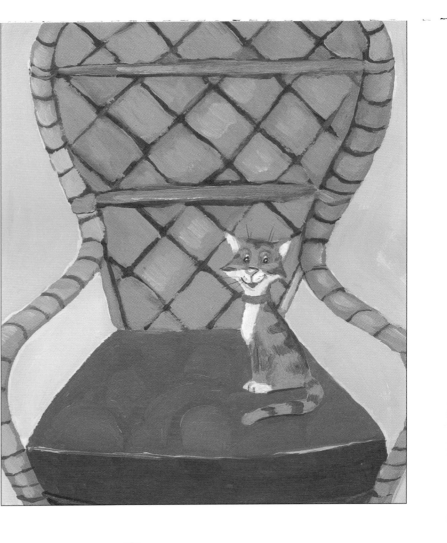

Cat sat.

Tap, tap.

The cats sat.

Fold

Ffft! Cat tags Sal!

Tag!

Lada Kratky

This book belongs to:

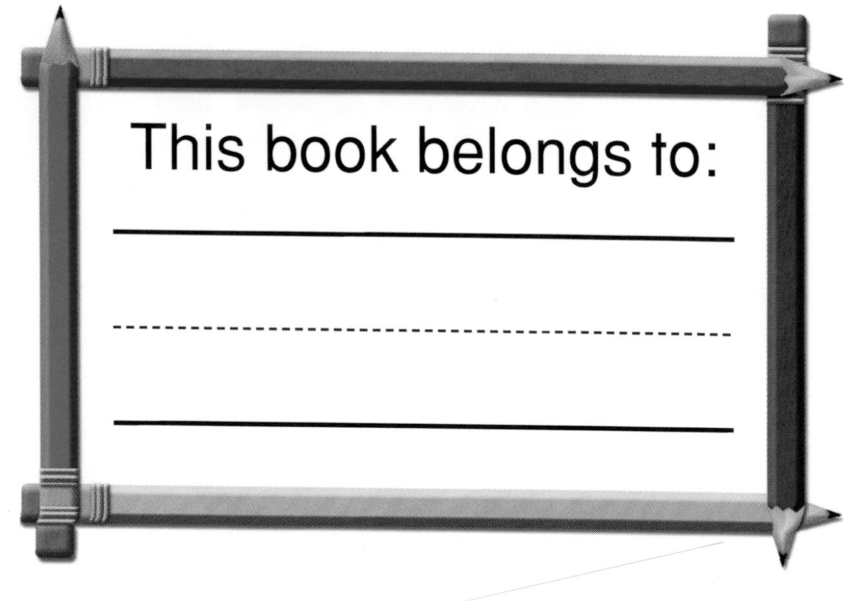

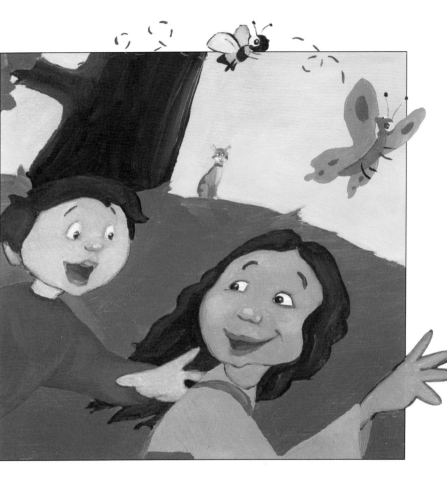

Sal tags Cat.

Sam tags Pat.

Pat tags Sal.

Sal has rags!

Rags

Lada Kratky

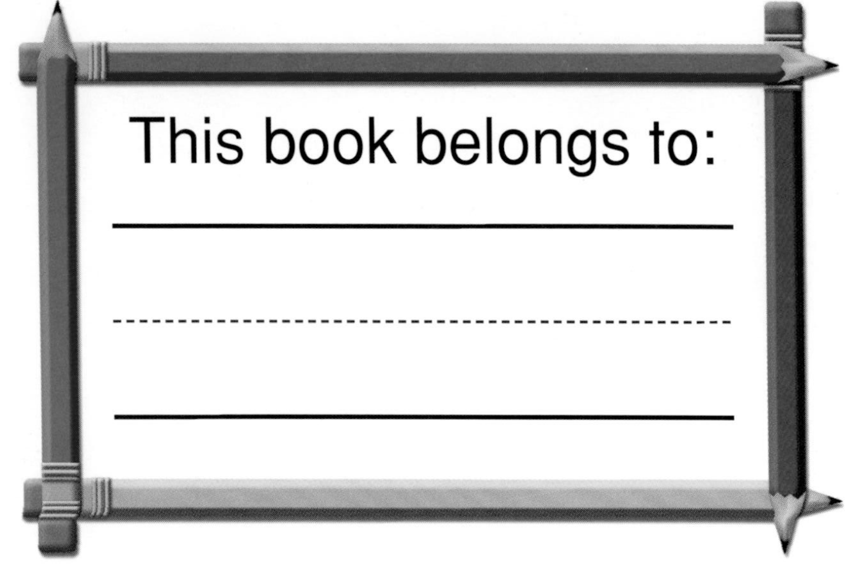
This book belongs to:

Cat has a rag.

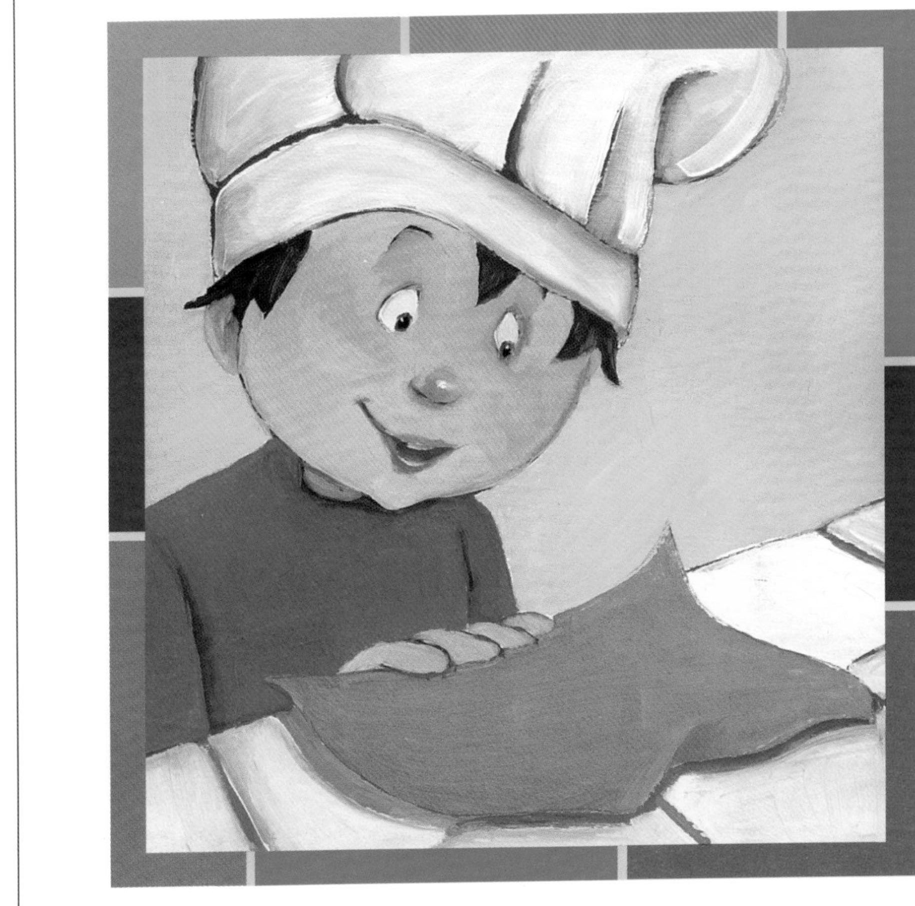

Sam has a rag.

Pam has a rag.

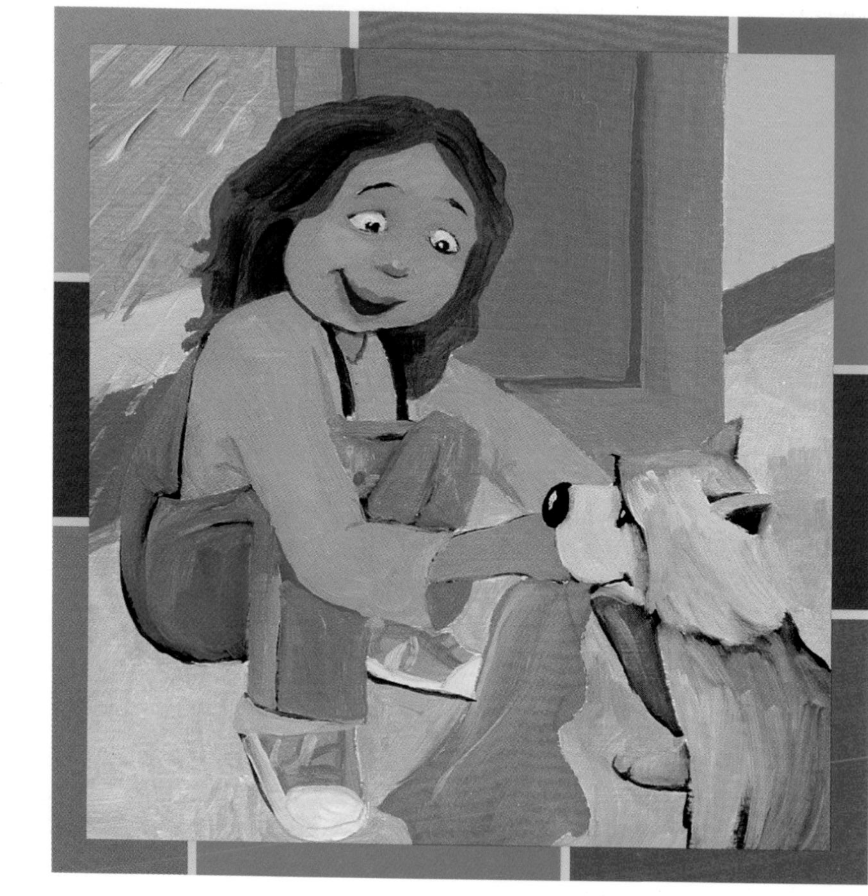

Pat has a rag.

Dad pets Ted.

Dad and Ted

Lada Kratky

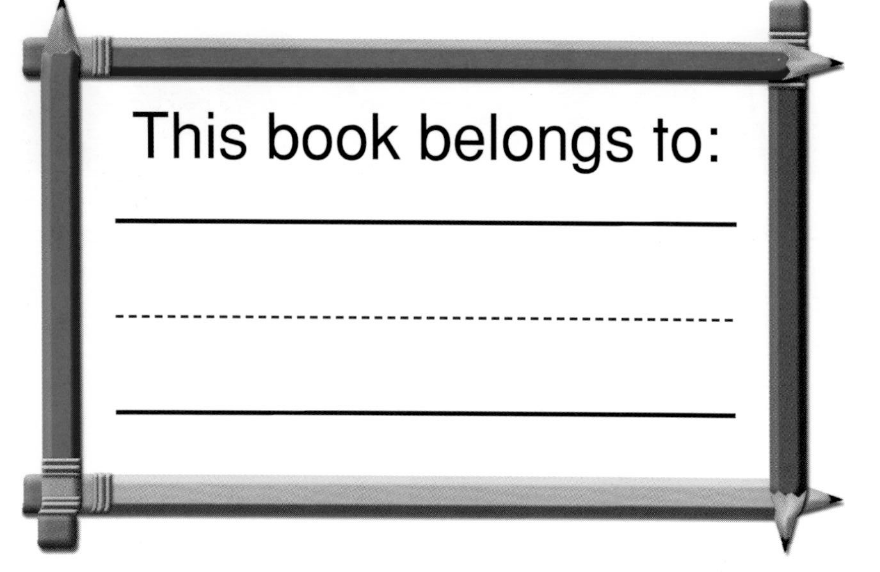

Ted pets Dad.

Ted is sad.

Dad is mad.

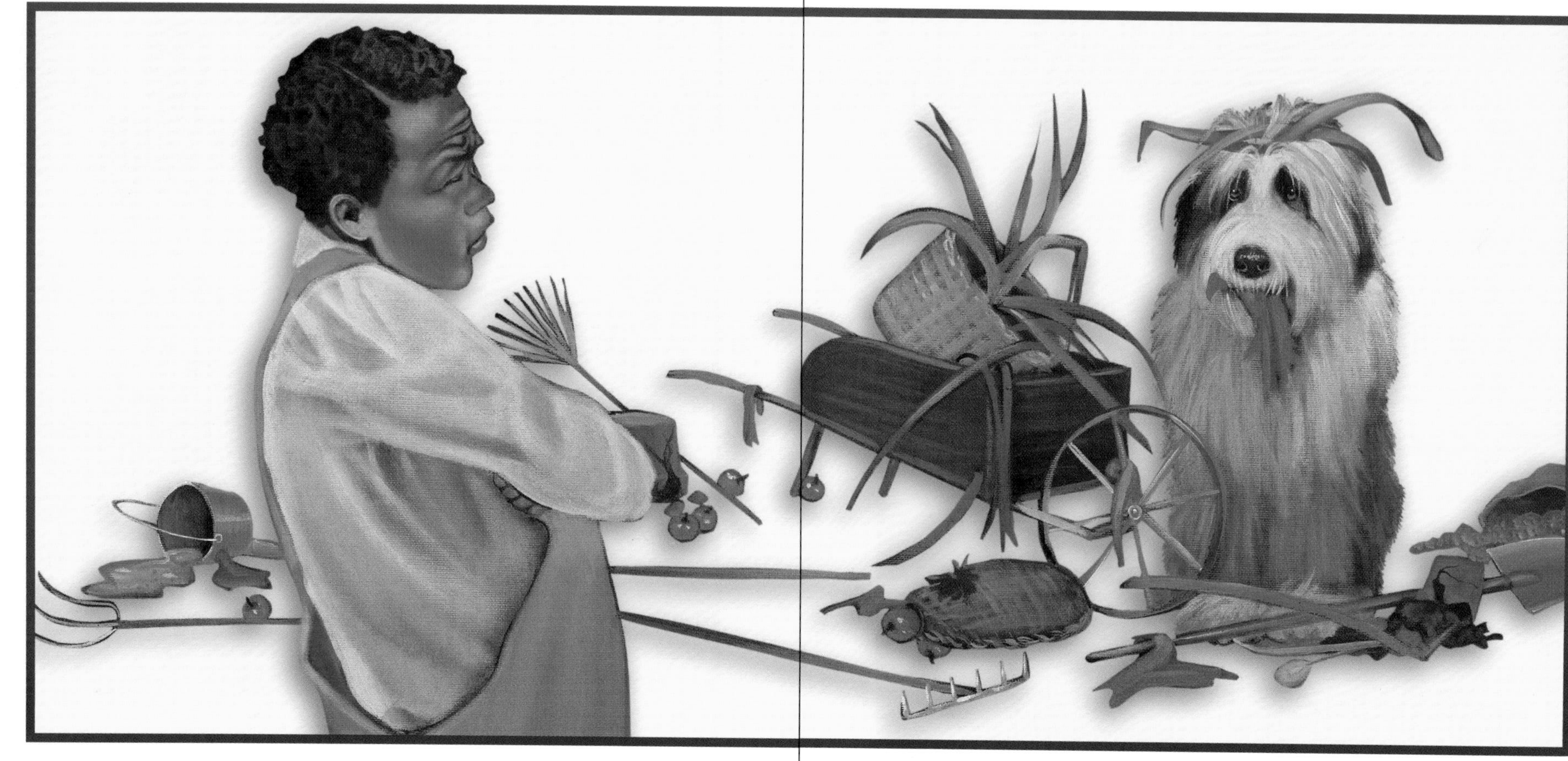

Dad is mad at Ted.

ham and eggs.

Pets

Lada Kratky

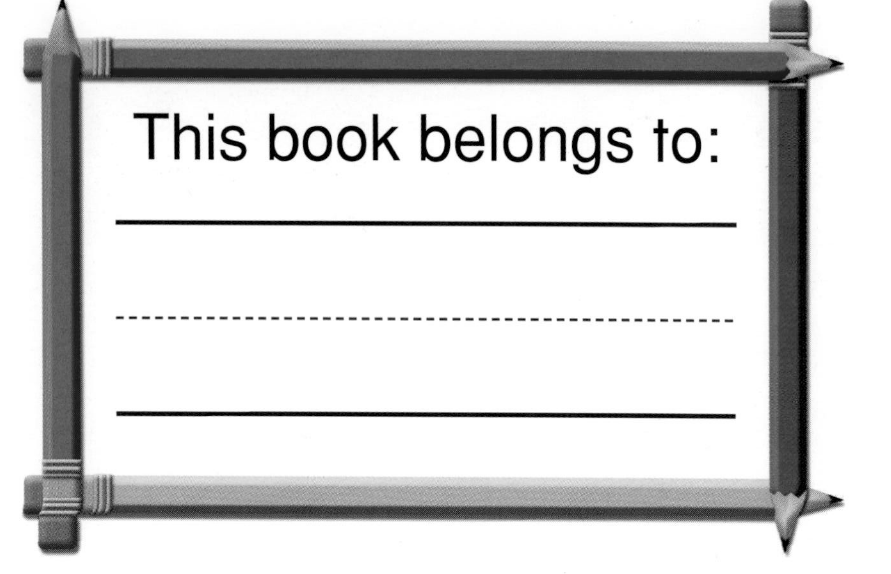

This book belongs to:

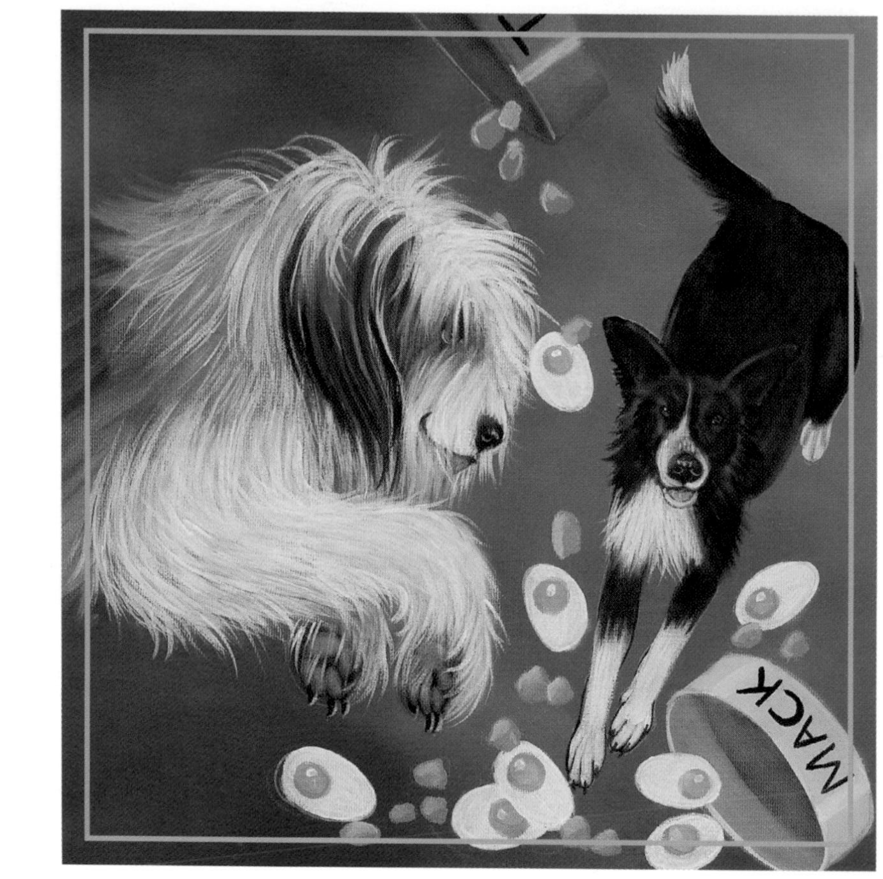

The pets get . . .

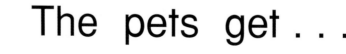

Mack gets eggs.

Ted gets fed.

Mack gets fed.

Ted gets ham.

Ted and the hen ran.

The Nap

Lada Kratky

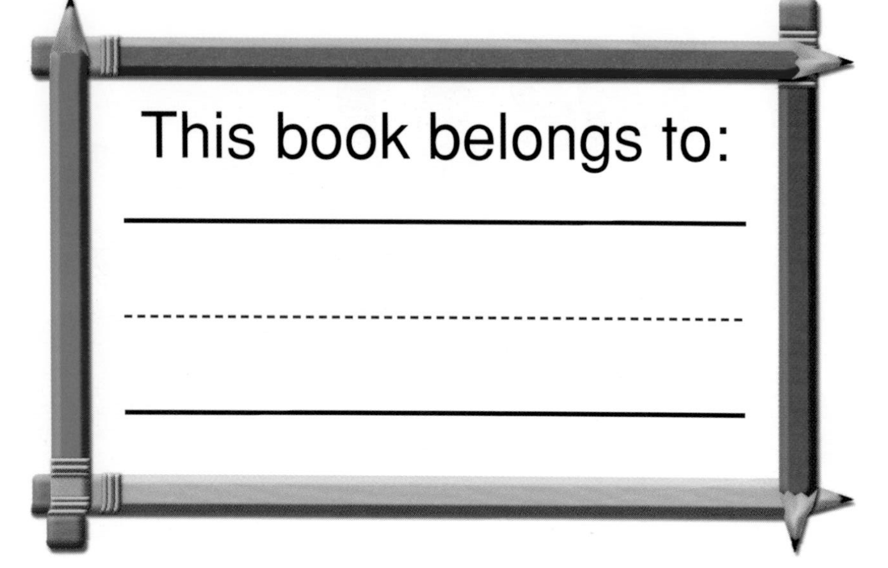

Peg fell. The cat fell.

Peg goes!

The Red Van

Lada Kratky

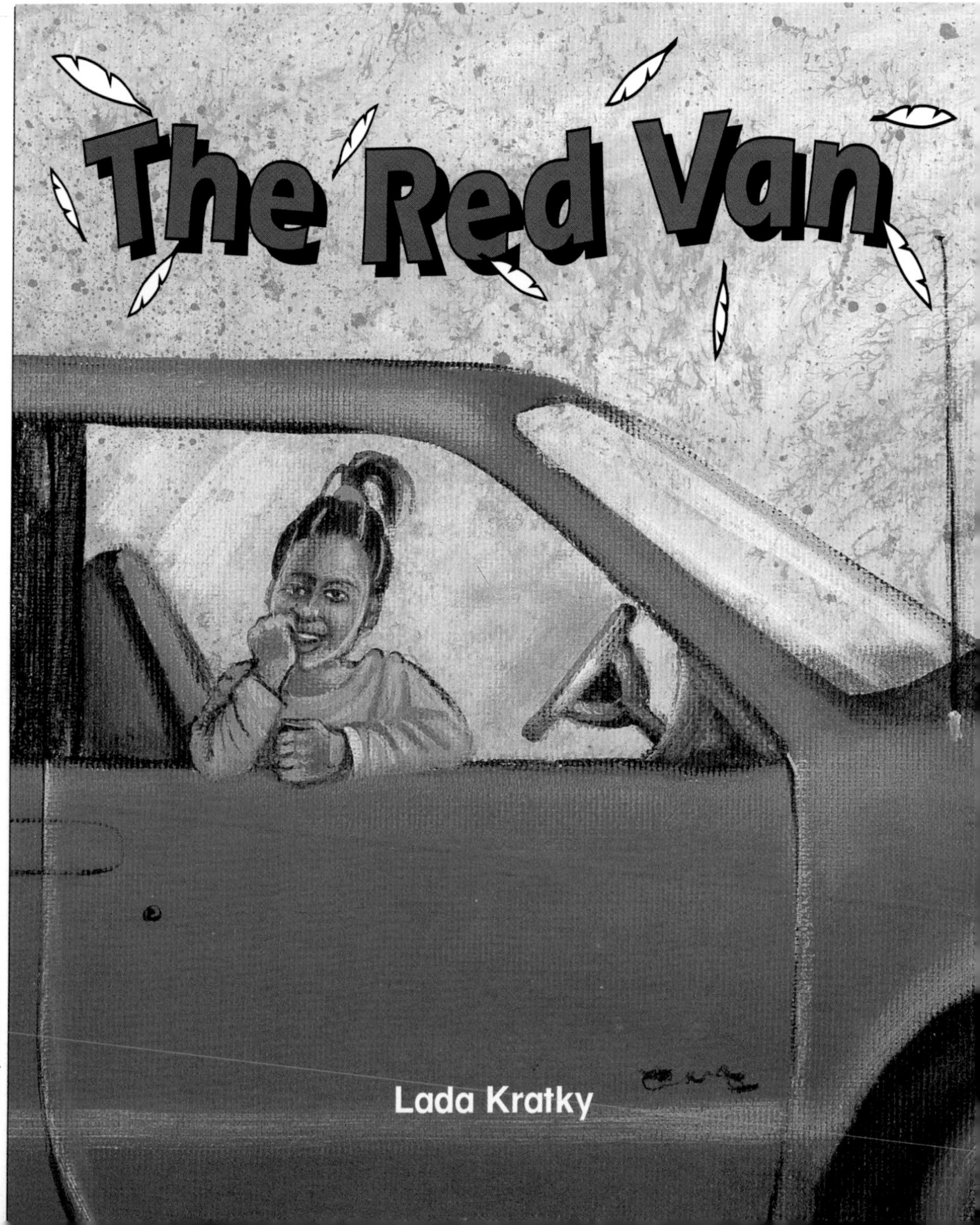

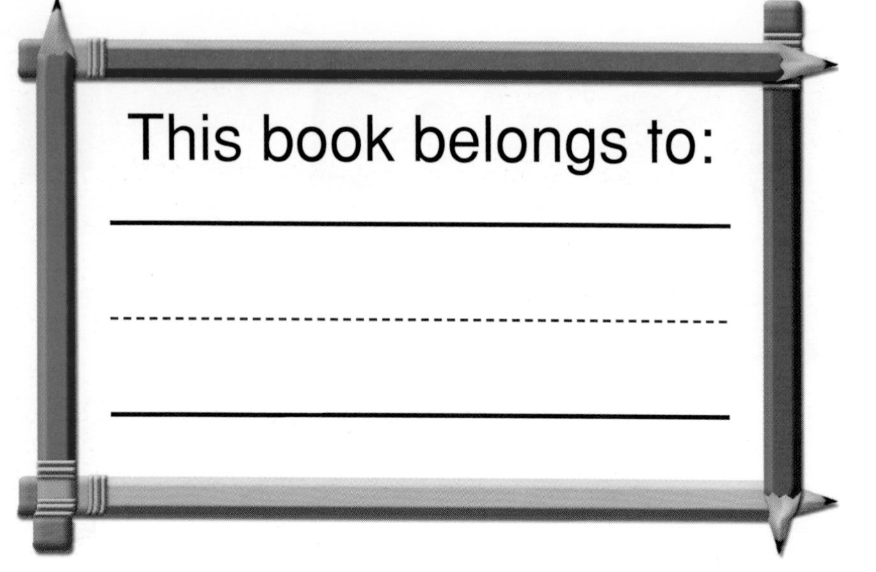

Ten hens get in.

Ted ran.

Peg had a nap.

A cat had a nap.

A hen had a nap.

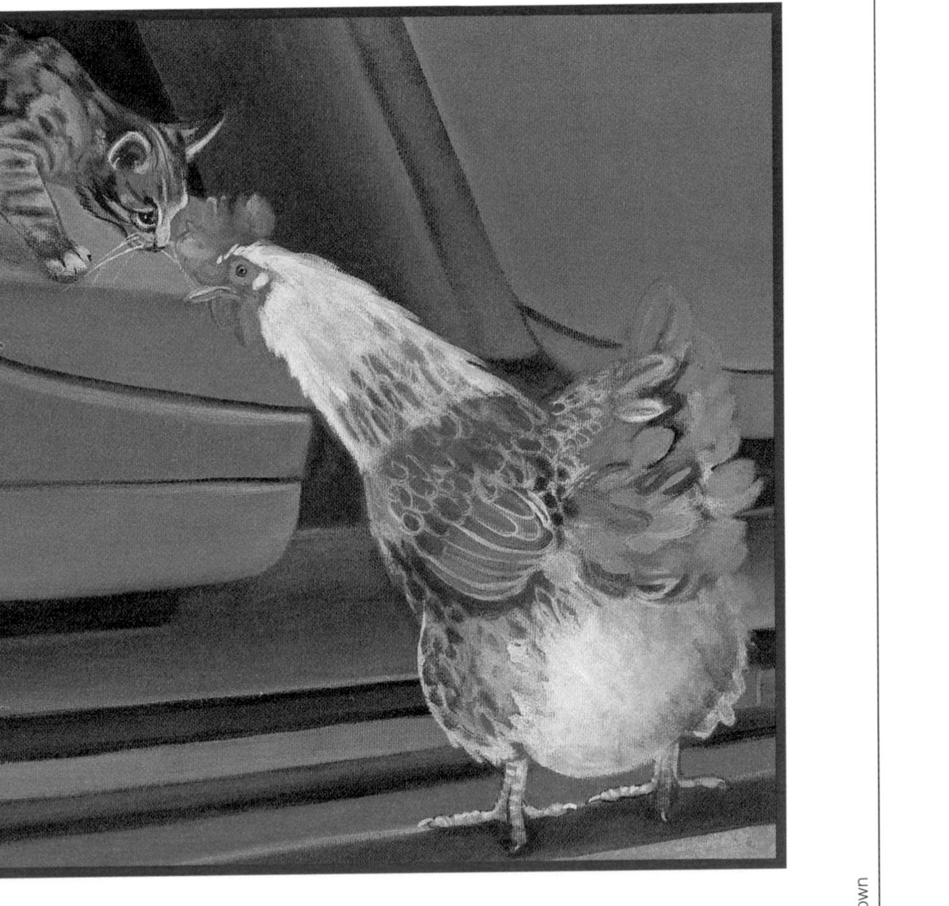

A hen gets in.

Peg is in the van.

A cat gets in.

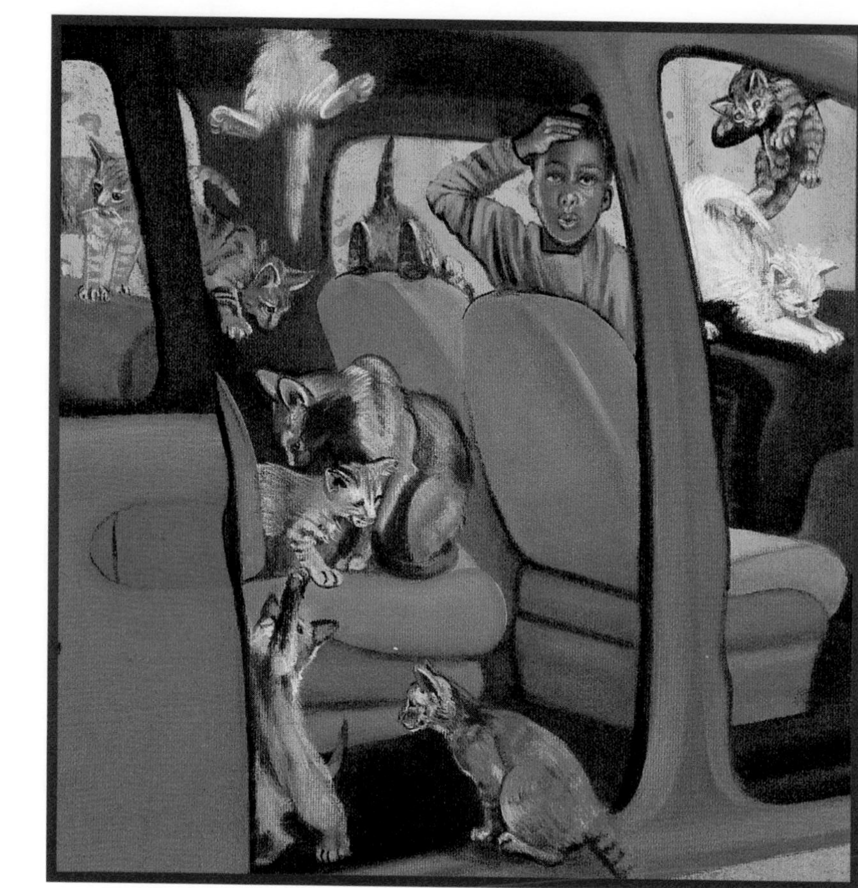

Ten cats get in.

I get to the top.

Dog and I

Lada Kratky

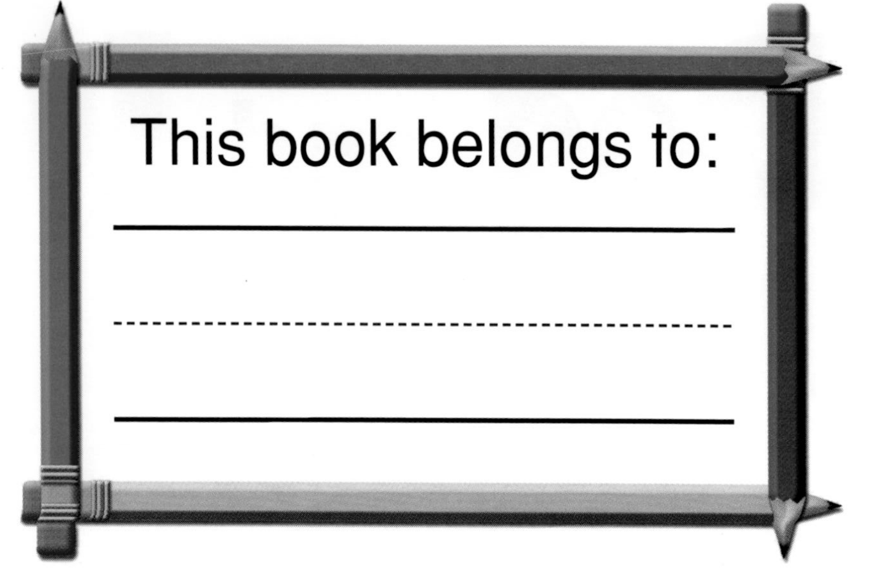

Dog goes fast.

I take off.

Dog can jog.

I can jog.

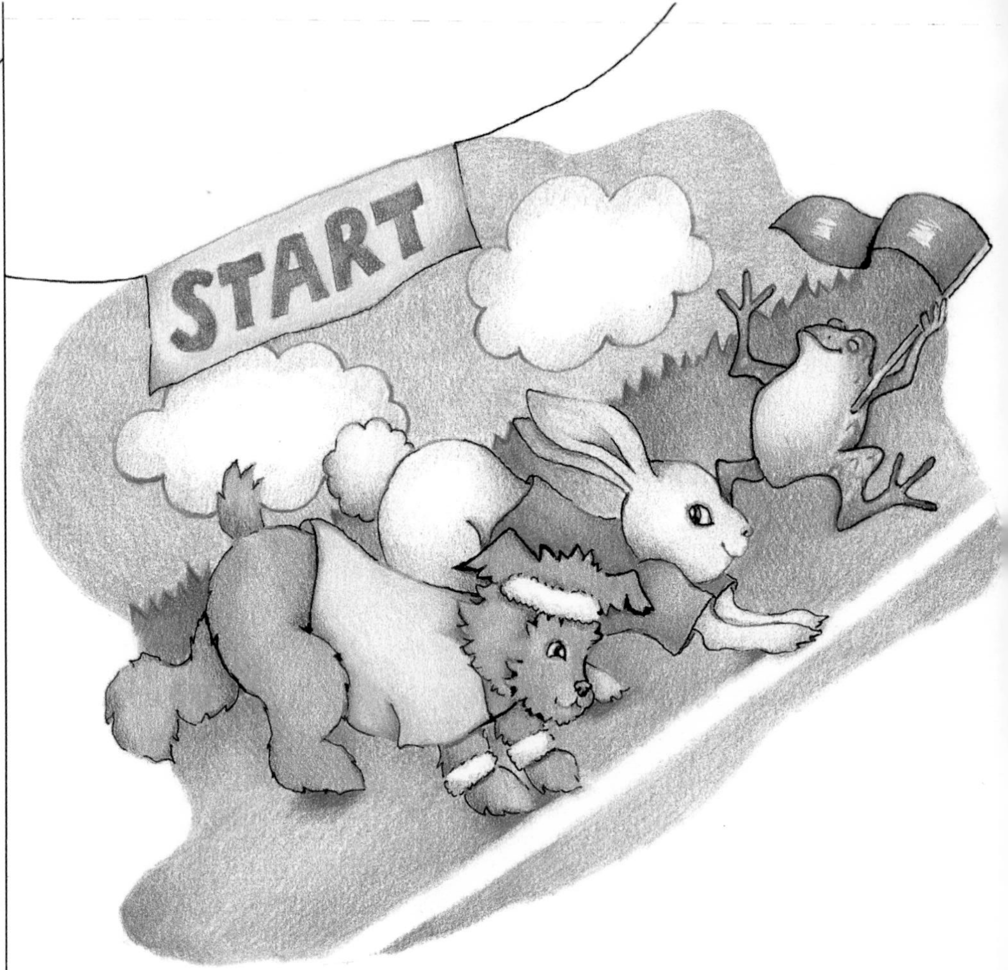

Dog and I get set.

Bam!

The Toss

Lada Kratky

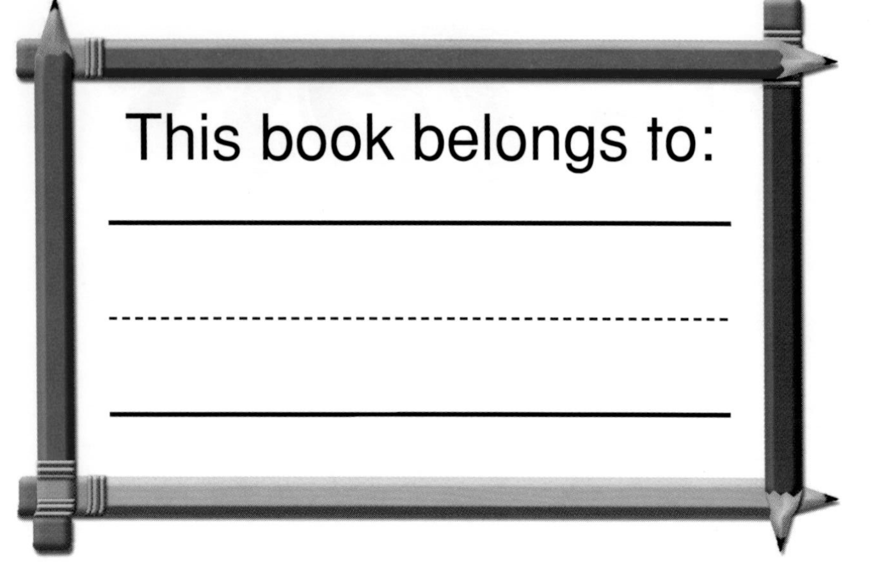

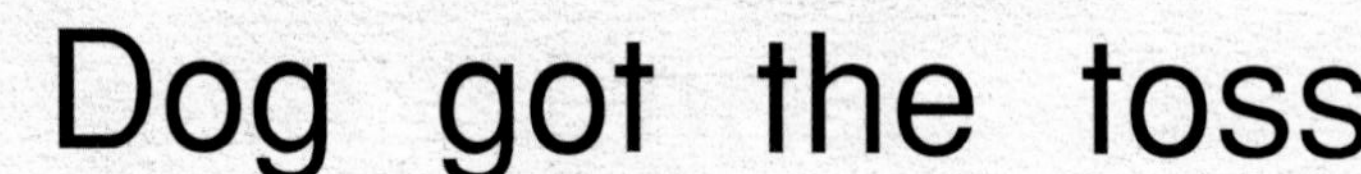

Dog got the toss.

Dog got a cap.

Dog got a bat.

Dog got set.

Pig can not zag!

Zig Zig Pig

Lada Kratky

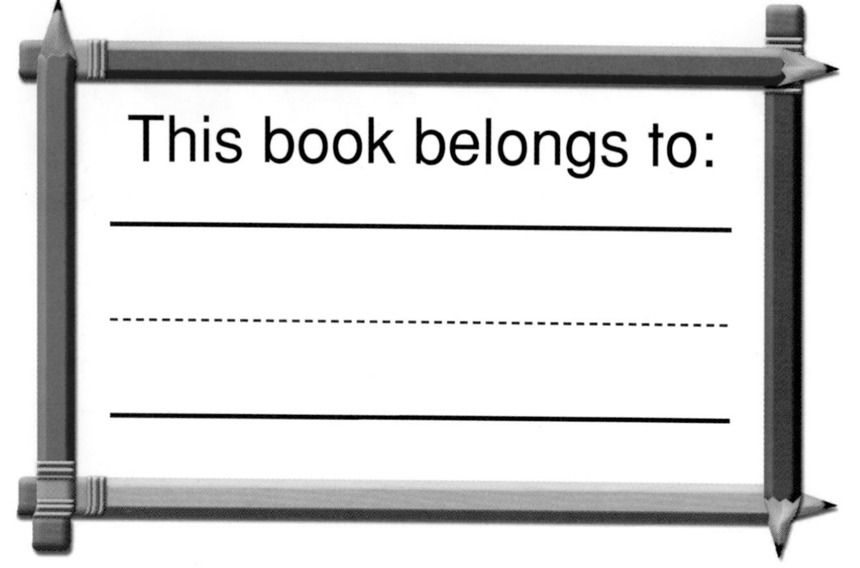

Zig...zig...zig.

Pig can zig.

Dad can zig.

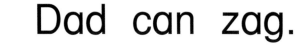

Dad can zag.

Dad can zig
and zag.

Look at the Q
on Pig!

Look at the Q

Lada Kratky

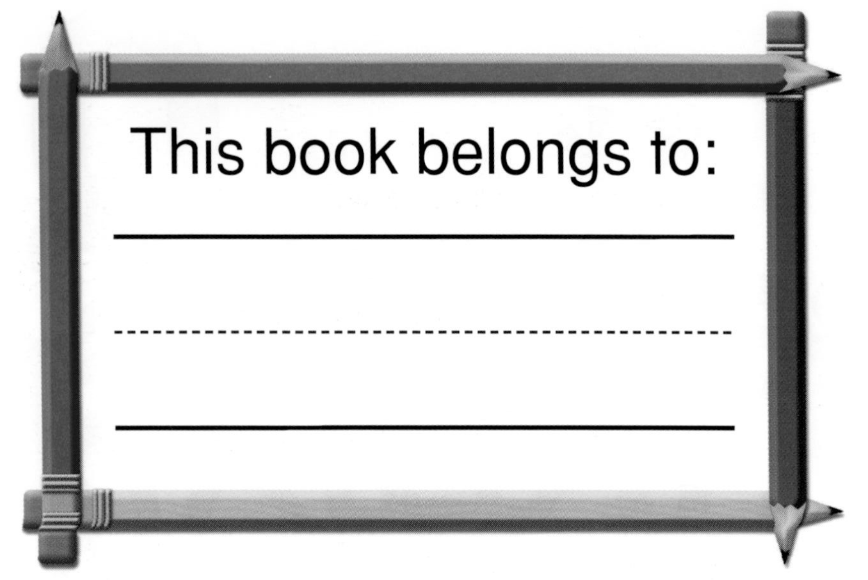

BAM!

Look at the Q

on the pen.

Look at the Q

on the hat.

Look at the Q
on the bin.

Look at the Q
on the bag.

Fox did not get in!

Yip! Yip!

Fox and Pig

Lada Kratky

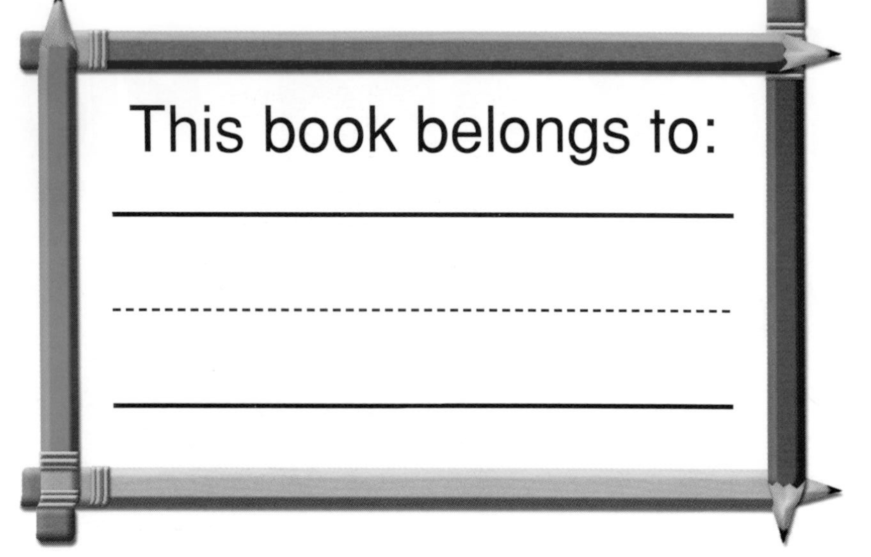

Pig hid in a box.

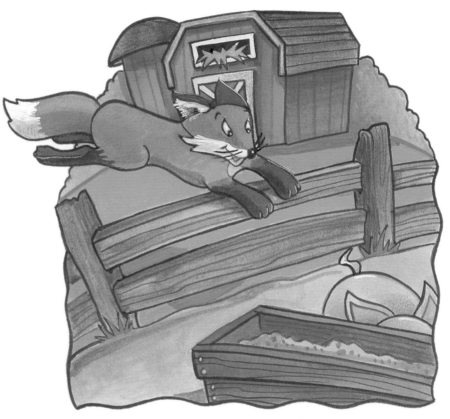

Fox ran and ran.

Pig ran and ran.

The sun is hot.

I will hop in!

Fill It Up

Lada Kratky

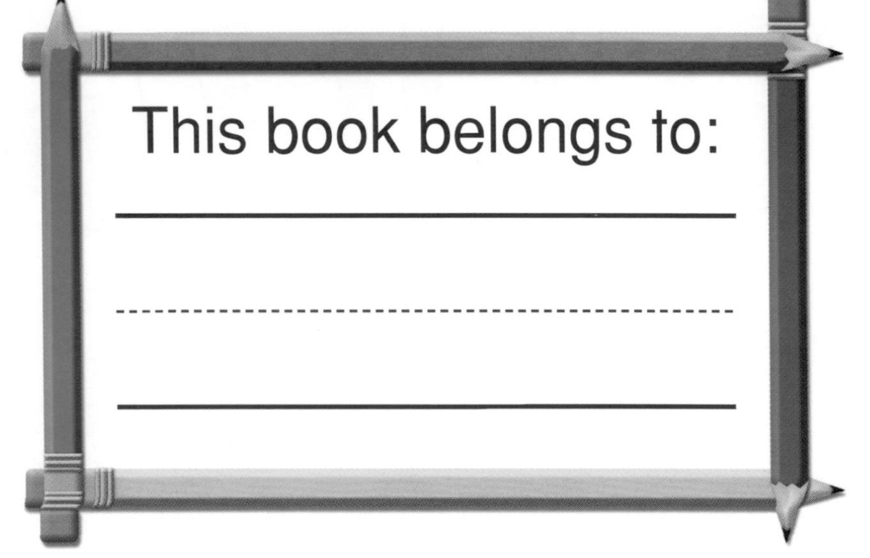

I will fill up
the jug.

The sun is hot.

Hop in, Max!

I will fill up

the cup.

The sun is hot.
Hop in, Bug!

I will fill up
the pan.

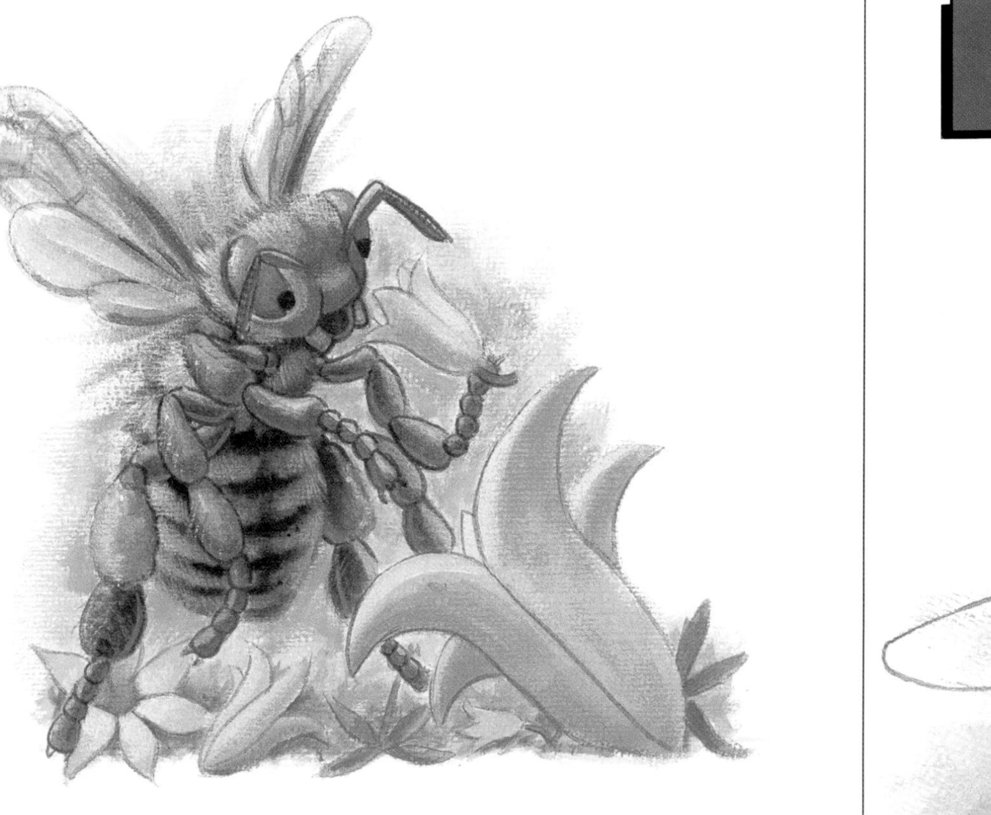

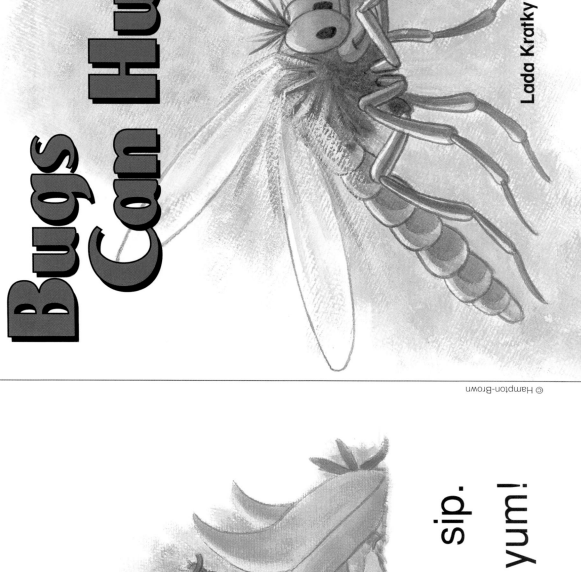

A bug can sip.
M-m-m-m, yum!

Bugs Can Hum

Lada Kratky

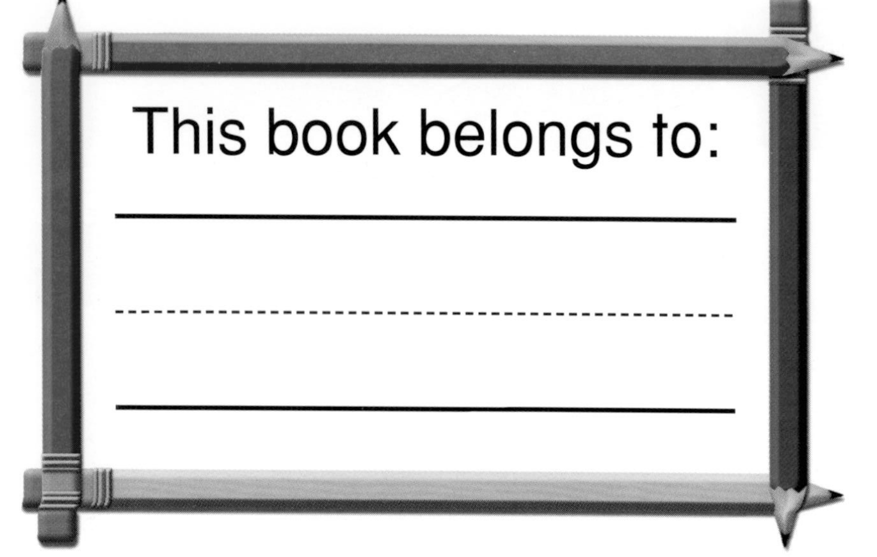

A bug can dig.

Ug!

A bug can jog.

Huff, puff!

A bug can hum.

Hum-m-m-m!

A bug can run.

Huff, huff!

A bug can hop.

Puff, puff!